444+ Fun Fascinating Train Facts for Kids Ages 8–12:

Discover Locomotives, Bullet Trains, Subways, and More with Trivia, Quizzes, and Amazing Pictures!

Dr. Rabea Hadi
Board Certified Family Physician
Medical Scholar and Academic Trainer
Author of "Choose Your Quest" Series

Table of Contents

Disclaimer
Your Exclusive Adventure Awaits!

Chapter 1: The First Trains in History
Chapter 2: Steam-Powered Giants
Chapter 3: Trains Around the World
Chapter 4: Record-Breaking Trains
Chapter 5: Subway Secrets
Chapter 6: Bullet Trains and High-Speed Marvels
Chapter 7: Train Jobs – Engineers, Conductors, and More
Chapter 8: Crazy Cargo – What Trains Carry
Chapter 9: Famous Train Rides
Chapter 10: Train Disasters and Heroic Rescues
Chapter 11: Animal Passengers and Funny Incidents
Chapter 12: Train Technology – Wheels, Tracks & Signals
Chapter 13: Famous Train Stations
Chapter 14: Ice, Snow, and Mountain Rails
Chapter 15: Eco-Friendly and Solar Trains
Chapter 16: The Future of Trains – Hovering and Flying?
Chapter 17: Train Travel Tips and Safety Facts for Kids
Chapter 18: Mini Train Challenges, Records, and World Trivia
Bonus Chapter: The Ultimate Train Trivia Challenge!
☐ THANK YOU!

About the Author: The Mind Behind the Initiative of Laughter and Learning

Books for Teens & Adults

Choose Your Quest: The Dwarven Jester Spy: An Interactive Hilarious High Fantasy Espionage Adventure

Fiction for Children

Fun Facts For Sports Kids (21 book series)

Did You Know That Your Heart Beats Over 100,000 Times a Day or That Stars Can Be Different Colors?

Disclaimer

Information in this book is for education and entertainment purposes. For any mental, medical or financial advice, please consult a licensed professional.

By reading this book, you agree that under no circumstances is the author responsible for any losses that are incurred due to using information within.

This is a work of fiction. Names, characters, places, and incidents either are products of the author's imagination or are used fictitiously. Any resemblance to actual persons, living or dead, events, or locales is entirely coincidental.

Copyright © 2025 Dr. Rabea Hadi

All rights reserved.

No part of this book may be reproduced, stored in a retrieval system, or transmitted in any form or by any means, electronic, mechanical, photocopying, recording, or otherwise, without the prior written permission of the publisher and author, Dr. Rabea Hadi

I appreciate your constructive feedback at

mail@chooseyourquest.net & review at your preferred store.

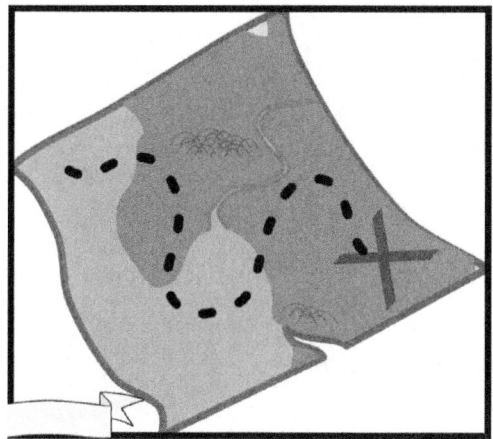

444+ FUN AND FASCINATING TRAIN FACTS for Kids Ages 8-12

Discover Locomotives, Bullet Trains, Subways, and More with Trivia, Quizzes, and Amazing Pictures!

Your Exclusive Adventure Awaits!

Dear Fellow Adventurer,

Thank you for navigating the twists and turns of my books! As a token of appreciation, I'm thrilled to offer you an exclusive, funny, and interactive short story set in the whimsical world of *Choose Your Quest*. It's available only to my most kind (and supportive) readers like you?

Why Choose My Books?
Are you tired of books filled with harmful messages, profanity, or bad values? Do you want something lighthearted yet meaningful for your child—content that teaches good values while being fun and engaging?

I believe what our children read shapes their future—and our world. That's why I craft clean, fun, and educational stories. Whether I'm caring for patients in my clinic or crafting new adventures, my mission is the same: spreading kindness, good values, and a love for learning through clean humor and storytelling.

Join the Quest for Clean Fun!
By subscribing to my website **ChooseYourQuest.net**, you may get:

- Access to free promos of my books occasionally.
- Guaranteed clean and fun content for readers of all ages.

- Updates on my latest projects (no spam, ever—I promise!).

Scan the QR code to claim your exclusive short story from all books section, and join our band of adventurers. Together, let's make learning and laughter universal!

Your thoughts matter to me! Share your feedback at **mail@chooseyourquest.net**. Let's build a better, cleaner, and more fun reading experience for everyone!

ADVENTURE

Introduction

Dear Young Train Explorer,

Welcome aboard!

Have you ever wondered what makes a bullet train so fast? Or how a train can glide above the ground without wheels? Maybe you've seen a subway zoom by or heard a whistle in the distance and thought, "How do trains do that?"

Well, wonder no more—this book is packed with **fun facts, cool stories, awesome pictures, and quick quizzes** to test your train brain!

You'll travel around the world, deep underground, up snowy mountains, and even into the future of transportation. You'll meet famous trains, smart engineers and powerful engines.

So grab your conductor's cap and get ready to explore the thrilling, surprising, and totally true world of trains!

Are you ready to ride? Let's go!

Chapter 1: The First Trains in History

1. The first full-size steam locomotive was built in 1804 by an inventor named Richard Trevithick.

2. Early trains were mostly used to carry coal and iron from mines to factories.

3. The very first tracks weren't metal—they were stone grooves in Ancient Greece!

4. Before steam engines, horses pulled small carts on tracks.

5. The famous "Tom Thumb" was the first American-built steam locomotive, created in 1830.

6. Trains became faster and more powerful as engineers improved their designs.

7. Early steam locomotives used coal and water to create power.

8. The wheels of trains were designed to fit snugly on tracks, keeping them from slipping.

9. The first train passengers rode in open-air carriages.

10. England had one of the earliest passenger train systems in the 1820s.

11. The Stockton and Darlington Railway in England was the first public railway to use steam engines.

12. George Stephenson improved train designs and made them more reliable.

13. **His famous locomotive, the "Rocket," reached speeds of 30 mph (48 km/h) in 1829!**

14. Trains helped spark the Industrial Revolution by moving materials quickly.

15. By the 1850s, trains were connecting entire countries.

16. Early train whistles warned people and animals that a train was coming.

17. Trains were sometimes called "iron horses."

18. Locomotives could weigh more than 40 tons (36,000 kg) even in the 1800s!

19. Building train tracks through mountains and rivers was a huge challenge.

20. Steam trains needed constant stops for water and coal.

21. Some early passengers were scared of the new "speed machines."

22. Trains brought jobs, travel, and new opportunities to small towns.

23. Railway stations became busy centers of life in cities.

24. Trains helped mail and newspapers travel faster than ever before.

25. The invention of trains changed the world forever.

Quiz Time: Multiple Choice Questions

1. Who built the first full-size steam locomotive?
A. George Stephenson
B. Richard Trevithick
C. Thomas Edison
D. James Watt

2. What pulled carts before steam engines were invented?
A. Tractors
B. Robots
C. Horses
D. Camels

3. What was the name of the first American steam locomotive?
A. Rocket
B. Lightning
C. Iron Runner
D. Tom Thumb

✓ MCQ Answer Key

1 – B
2 – C
3 – D

Chapter 2: Steam-Powered Giants

1. Steam trains were the most powerful machines of their time during the 1800s.

2. They used fire to heat water in a boiler, turning it into steam.

3. The steam pushed pistons that turned the wheels of the train.

4. Some steam locomotives had over **1,000 horsepower**!

5. The larger the boiler, the more powerful the train.

6. Engineers had to constantly shovel coal into the firebox to keep the train running.

7. It could take **two people** just to operate one steam engine.

8. Steam engines made loud hissing sounds and released big clouds of smoke.

9. Some steam locomotives had giant wheels over **6 feet (1.8 meters)** tall.

10. The famous "Big Boy" locomotive built in the 1940s was over **132 feet (40 meters)** long.

11. "Big Boy" could pull more than 4,000 tons of cargo!

12. Steam trains had whistles that engineers used to signal other workers.

13. The steam whistle sound became a symbol of the industrial age.

14. Trains needed strong tracks made of steel to carry their weight.

15. Steam engines worked best on flat land but could climb small hills.

16. Some trains used water towers placed along the tracks to refill their tanks.

17. A fully loaded steam engine could weigh more than **600,000 pounds (272,000 kg)**.

18. Railroads hired firemen to manage the fire and keep pressure steady.

19. Steam locomotives had large headlights to see at night.

20. Some engines had cowcatchers in the front to clear debris from the tracks.

21. The steam train's chugging rhythm came from its pistons working back and forth.

22. The inside of the locomotive was hot, loud, and full of moving parts.

23. Early train engineers had to be very skilled and alert.

24. Steam locomotives needed lots of maintenance and cleaning.

25. Although they're mostly retired now, some steam trains still run for tourists and fun!

Quiz Time: Multiple Choice Questions

1. What did steam trains burn to make steam?
A. Wood
B. Gasoline
C. Coal
D. Oil

2. How tall were the biggest train wheels?
A. 2 feet
B. 4 feet
C. 6 feet
D. 10 feet

3. What was the name of the huge steam locomotive built in the 1940s?
A. Rocket
B. Big Thunder
C. Big Boy
D. Iron Giant

✓ MCQ Answer Key

1 – C
2 – C
3 – C

Chapter 3: Trains Around the World

1. Japan is famous for its super-fast bullet trains called **Shinkansen**.

2. These trains can travel at speeds over **200 mph (320 km/h)**.

3. In France, the **TGV** (Train à Grande Vitesse) holds speed records for passenger trains.

4. India's rail network is one of the **largest in the world**, with over 65,000 km of track.

5. The **Trans-Siberian Railway** in Russia is the longest railway line—over **5,700 miles (9,200 km)** long.

6. In Australia, the **Indian Pacific** train travels from coast to coast.

7. Germany is known for its **ICE trains**, which are sleek, fast, and futuristic.

8. In China, high-speed trains connect major cities in just a few hours.

9. Africa's rail systems are expanding with new electric trains in places like Morocco and Kenya.

10. The **Eurostar** travels under the English Channel through a tunnel connecting England and France.

11. In Switzerland, mountain trains climb through steep and snowy areas using special gears.

12. Canada's **VIA Rail** offers beautiful rides through forests and mountains.

13. Brazil has trains that carry people deep into the Amazon rainforest.

14. In the U.S., **Amtrak** trains connect over 500 destinations.

15. Mexico's new **Maya Train** project aims to bring fast trains across tourist areas.

16. In the Netherlands, electric trains run on wind-powered electricity.

17. The Hejaz Railway was the first major railway in the Muslim world, built by the Ottoman Empire from 1900–1908. It connected Damascus to Medina to help pilgrims travel for Hajj to worship Allah the most merciful. Funded by Muslims worldwide, it used steam trains and symbolized unity and progress in the Islamic world.

18. Egypt still uses train routes originally built over 100 years ago.

19. Some cities in South Korea have fully automated trains without drivers!

20. In Italy, the **Frecciarossa** is a stylish red train that zooms through cities.

21. South Africa's **Blue Train** is a luxury train with 5-star service.

22. New Zealand trains often pass through volcanoes, lakes, and green valleys.

23. Indonesia's trains connect busy cities across thousands of islands.

24. Argentina has old-style trains that still carry passengers across rural lands.

25. Trains help connect people across every continent except **Antarctica**.

Quiz Time: Multiple Choice Questions

1. What is the name of Japan's high-speed trains?
A. ICE
B. Shinkansen
C. Eurostar
D. Rocket Train

2. Which country has the longest railway line in the world?
A. China

B. United States
C. Russia
D. India

3. What continent does not have any trains?
A. Australia
B. Africa
C. South America
D. Antarctica

✓ MCQ Answer Key

1 – B
2 – C
3 – D

Chapter 4: Record-Breaking Trains

1. The **fastest train** in the world is Japan's **Maglev**, reaching speeds of **375 mph (603 km/h)** during testing.

2. The longest train ever recorded was in Australia, made up of **682 cars** and stretching over **4.5 miles (7.3 km)**!

3. The **heaviest train** carried nearly **100,000 tons** of iron ore in South Africa.

4. The **steepest passenger train** route is the Pilatus Railway in Switzerland, with a gradient of 48%!

5. The **highest railway** in the world is the **Qinghai–Tibet Railway** in China, reaching over **16,600 feet (5,072 m)**.

6. The **coldest place** where trains run year-round is Siberia, where temperatures can drop below **-60°F (-51°C)**.

7. The **hottest train route** runs through the Australian Outback, where temps can reach over **120°F (49°C)**.

8. The **oldest working steam engine** still running is over **150 years old**!

9. The **busiest train station** in the world is **Shinjuku Station** in Tokyo, Japan, serving over **3 million people daily**.

10. The **longest tunnel** for trains is the **Gotthard Base Tunnel** in Switzerland—**35 miles (57 km)** long.

11. The **fastest subway train** operates in Seoul, South Korea, hitting speeds of **75 mph (120 km/h)**.

12. The **longest straight railway line** is in Australia—**297 miles (478 km)** with no curves!

13. The **most luxurious train** in the world is the **Maharajas' Express** in India.

14. The **first train to break 100 mph (160 km/h)** was the British locomotive **Flying Scotsman**.

15. The **quietest high-speed train** is France's **TGV**, using special track and wheels.

16. The **oldest underground metro** system is London's, opened in **1863**.

17. The **first electric train** was built in **1879** in Germany.

18. The **most countries crossed by one train ride** is the Trans-Siberian route—connecting Europe and Asia.

19. The **longest suspension railway** is in Wuppertal, Germany, where the train hangs

under the track.

20. The **fastest scheduled train ride** today is between **Beijing and Shanghai**, taking just **4.5 hours**.

21. The **heaviest snowfall train line** is in Japan, with snow walls over **20 feet (6 meters)** high.

22. The **tallest railway bridge** is in India—the **Chenab Bridge**, taller than the Eiffel Tower!

23. The **most loops in a railway** track can be found in India's Darjeeling Himalayan Railway.

24. The **highest-speed crash-test** for a train reached over 100 mph (160 km/h) for safety testing.

25. The **most photographed train** in the world is the **Glenfinnan Viaduct** train in Scotland, featured in many travel ads and films.

Quiz Time: Multiple Choice Questions

1. What is the fastest train in the world?
A. TGV
B. Maglev
C. Shinkansen
D. Amtrak Acela

2. Which train crosses the highest railway in the world?
A. Eurostar
B. Indian Pacific

C. Qinghai–Tibet Railway
D. Trans-Amazon Express

3. Where is the world's longest straight railway line?
A. Canada
B. United States
C. Russia
D. Australia

✓ **MCQ Answer Key**

1 – B
2 – C
3 – D

Chapter 5: Subway Secrets

1. The very first subway system opened in **London in 1863**.

2. London's subway is also called "The Tube" because of its round tunnels.

3. New York City has one of the **largest subway systems** in the world.

4. The NYC subway has **472 stations**—more than any other city.

5. Subway trains run **underground**, but some parts travel above ground too.

6. The **deepest subway station** is in Pyongyang, North Korea, over **360 feet (110 meters)** deep.

7. Seoul's subway has **Wi-Fi** and touchscreen maps on board!

8. Tokyo's subways are famous for being extremely **clean and efficient**.

9. Moscow's subway stations look like **underground palaces**, with marble walls and chandeliers.

10. Paris's subway is called the **"Métro"** and is known for its artsy station designs.

11. Some subways have **platform screen doors** to protect passengers.

12. The average subway train travels at about **30 mph (48 km/h)**.

13. Subways help reduce city traffic by carrying thousands of people at once.

14. Some modern subway trains are **driverless** and fully automated.

15. Many subways use **electric power** from rails beneath the train.

16. The first U.S. subway opened in **Boston in 1897**.

17. Most subway cars are made from **aluminum or stainless steel** to stay strong and light.

18. Singapore's subway trains have **no chewing gum allowed** rules!

19. The **quietest subways** use rubber tires instead of metal wheels.

20. Subways often run 24 hours in big cities like New York.

21. Some cities have **underground shopping malls** connected to subway stations.

22. Subway maps are **color-coded** to help riders find their way easily.

23. Trains in large cities can arrive every **2 to 3 minutes** during rush hour.

24. Escalators in some subway systems are over **200 feet (60 meters)** long!

25. Subway trains help reduce pollution by replacing thousands of cars on the road.

Quiz Time: Multiple Choice Questions

1. What was the first city to have a subway system?
A. New York
B. Moscow
C. Paris
D. London

2. What do some subways use instead of metal wheels to make less noise?
A. Wood
B. Plastic
C. Rubber tires
D. Sponges

3. Which subway system has the most stations in the world?
A. Tokyo
B. New York City
C. London
D. Seoul

✓ MCQ Answer Key

1 – D
2 – C
3 – B

Chapter 6: Bullet Trains and High-Speed Marvels

1. **Bullet trains** are called that because of their sleek, pointed shape and amazing speed.

2. Japan's **Shinkansen** was the first bullet train, launched in **1964**.

3. Bullet trains can reach speeds over **200 mph (320 km/h)** in regular service.

4. The fastest bullet train in regular use is China's **Fuxing Hao**, reaching **217 mph (350 km/h)**.

5. Bullet trains ride on **special high-speed tracks** that are straighter and smoother than regular tracks.

6. Some bullet trains use **magnetic levitation (Maglev)**, allowing them to float slightly above the track.

7. Maglev trains reduce friction by **not touching the tracks at all**!

8. Bullet trains are incredibly **quiet**, even at high speeds.

9. They're designed to stay stable even during earthquakes in places like Japan.

10. In France, the **TGV** holds the world speed record for a wheeled train at **357 mph (575 km/h)**.

11. Germany's **ICE** trains are known for their comfort and speed.

12. South Korea's bullet trains are called **KTX**, connecting major cities quickly.

13. Italy's high-speed train is the **Frecciarossa**, or "Red Arrow."

14. Spain's **AVE** trains are super fast and cross the country from coast to coast.

15. Bullet trains can carry over **1,000 passengers** on a single trip.

16. The ride is so smooth that passengers can balance coins on tables!

17. Bullet trains often travel underground, through mountains, or on raised tracks.

18. Some bullet trains have **multiple classes**, like airplanes—economy, business, and premium.

19. The **driver's cabin** on a bullet train has high-tech controls and large viewing windows.

20. Bullet trains are more **energy efficient** than cars or planes.

21. Tickets can be reserved by **seat number**, just like airplanes.

22. Bullet trains rarely run late; Japan's average delay is less than **a minute per year**!

23. Some stations have **glass doors** that open in sync with the train.

24. Engineers constantly monitor tracks and systems for safety.

25. Bullet trains continue to improve, with future versions aiming for **500+ mph (800+ km/h)**!

Quiz Time: Multiple Choice Questions

1. What technology allows Maglev trains to float above the track?
A. Wind power
B. Solar panels
C. Magnetic levitation
D. Jet engines

2. Which country launched the first bullet train?
A. France

B. China
C. South Korea
D. Japan

3. What's the world speed record for a wheeled train?
A. 217 mph
B. 250 mph
C. 357 mph
D. 500 mph

✓ MCQ Answer Key

1 – C
2 – D
3 – C

Chapter 7: Train Jobs – Engineers, Conductors, and More

1. A **train engineer** is the person who drives the train and controls its speed and braking.

2. The **conductor** is in charge of the whole train, including the crew and passenger safety.

3. On freight trains, conductors check cargo, ensure secure loading, and manage paperwork.

4. **Rail yard workers** help connect and disconnect train cars.

5. **Switch operators** move the tracks to guide trains onto the right path.

6. **Signal operators** manage train lights and signs that tell trains when to stop or go.

7. **Inspectors** check the wheels, brakes, and engines to make sure everything works safely.

8. Some trains have **mechanical crews** that ride along in case repairs are needed.

9. **Station attendants** help passengers, sell tickets, and give directions.

10. **Train announcers** update riders with arrival and departure info.

11. **Cleaning crews** keep trains tidy between journeys.

12. On luxury or tourist trains, staff serve food and help with luggage.

13. **Train designers** are engineers who create new models of engines and cars.

14. **Track engineers** design and inspect the tracks for safety.

15. **Safety officers** investigate train incidents and make rules to prevent accidents.

16. High-speed trains require specially trained engineers with fast reflexes.

17. A **dispatcher** controls train traffic, like an air traffic controller for railroads.

18. Dispatchers monitor multiple trains at once using computers and cameras.

19. **Control centers** can track trains across entire countries in real-time.

20. In large cities, subway systems use **automated control rooms** to manage hundreds of trains.

21. Some trains now use **autopilot systems**, but staff are still needed onboard.

22. Train workers often wear **bright safety gear** to stay visible on tracks.

23. On freight trains, the crew may be just two people: an engineer and a conductor.

24. Train jobs often require special licenses and safety training.

25. Working on trains can be challenging but also exciting and rewarding!

Quiz Time: Multiple Choice Questions

1. Who is responsible for driving the train?
A. Conductor
B. Inspector

C. Dispatcher
D. Engineer

2. What does a dispatcher do?
A. Clean the train
B. Check tickets
C. Manage train traffic
D. Fix train wheels

3. Which worker checks if brakes and wheels are safe?
A. Conductor
B. Signal operator
C. Inspector
D. Attendant

✓ MCQ Answer Key

1 – D
2 – C
3 – C

Chapter 8: Crazy Cargo – What Trains Carry

1. Trains don't just carry people—they haul millions of tons of **cargo** every year.

2. **Freight trains** are designed to move goods, not passengers.

3. Some trains carry **coal**, used to power factories and power plants.

4. **Grain trains** transport corn, wheat, and other crops from farms to cities.

5. **Oil trains** move large tanks of fuel across countries.

6. Refrigerated cars, called **reefers**, keep food like milk and meat cold during transport.

7. **Auto trains** move brand-new cars from factories to dealerships.

8. Giant containers from ships are loaded onto **intermodal trains** for long-distance travel.

9. Some trains carry **logs and timber** for furniture and construction.

10. **Cement trains** deliver materials used to build roads and buildings.

11. Trains can even carry **airplanes**—at least their parts like wings and engines!

12. **Livestock trains** were once common, carrying cows, pigs, and sheep.

13. Today, animals are rarely moved by train, but it still happens in some places.

14. **Mail trains** used to sort and deliver letters while moving!

15. Some postal trains had onboard workers sorting mail by hand.

16. **Chemical trains** move important materials for factories and medicine.

17. **Military trains** carry tanks, trucks, and supplies for defense purposes.

18. Special armored trains have been used during wars to protect cargo.

19. **Garbage trains** help cities transport waste to distant landfills.

20. **Food trains** deliver rice, beans, sugar, and fruits across countries.

21. Some cargo trains are over **2 miles (3.2 km)** long!

22. Cranes at train yards lift containers off and place them onto trucks or ships.

23. **High-value trains** carry gold, electronics, or important equipment in secure cars.

24. Freight trains usually don't stop often—they go from point A to B without delays.

25. Without cargo trains, the world's economy would slow down a lot!

Quiz Time: Multiple Choice Questions

1. What kind of train keeps food cold while moving?
A. Reefer
B. Tanker
C. Hopper
D. Sleeper

2. Which of these is a cargo trains often move?
A. Tourists
B. Sound instruments
C. Livestock
D. Mail trucks

3. What do intermodal trains carry?
A. Passengers
B. Large containers
C. Gold bars
D. Books

✓ **MCQ Answer Key**

1 – A
2 – C
3 – B

Chapter 9: Famous Train Rides

1. The **Trans-Siberian Railway** is the longest passenger train ride in the world, running from Moscow to Vladivostok.

2. The **Orient Express** was a luxurious European train known for its fancy food and stylish cabins.

3. The **Rocky Mountaineer** in Canada takes passengers through snowy mountains and

forests.

4. **The Glacier Express** in Switzerland crosses high bridges and tunnels through the Alps.

5. The **Blue Train** in South Africa is a luxury ride with fine dining and private suites.

6. India's **Palace on Wheels** is decorated like royal palaces and offers full hotel service onboard.

7. The **Coast Starlight** in the U.S. goes along the West Coast with views of beaches, forests, and mountains.

8. The **Indian Pacific** crosses Australia from Sydney to Perth in a 4-day adventure.

9. Japan's **Narita Express** connects the airport to the center of Tokyo in high-speed style.

10. The **Bernina Express** in Switzerland climbs icy mountains and crosses over 190 bridges.

11. The **Eastern & Oriental Express** offers beautiful views between Thailand, Malaysia, and Singapore.

12. The **Jacobite Steam Train** in Scotland is the one shown crossing the famous Glenfinnan

Viaduct.

13. The **Ghan** crosses the Australian desert, from Darwin to Adelaide.

14. The **Royal Scotsman** is one of the most elegant trains in the UK.

15. The **California Zephyr** takes passengers from Chicago to San Francisco through the Rocky Mountains.

16. The **Eurostar** goes from London to Paris through the Channel Tunnel.

17. The **Tokaido Shinkansen** is Japan's busiest bullet train route, connecting Tokyo and Osaka.

18. The **Flåm Railway** in Norway is one of the steepest railways in the world.

19. The **Alaska Railroad** travels through snow, glaciers, and wild landscapes.

20. The **Sergei Eisenstein Express** in Russia features old-style Soviet decor.

21. The **Harz Narrow Gauge Railway** in Germany uses steam trains on mountain routes.

22. The **Lhasa Express** travels to Tibet at high altitudes.

23. The **Durango & Silverton Narrow Gauge Railroad** in Colorado offers a Wild West feel.

24. The **Maya Train** in Mexico is a new train being built to connect ancient ruins and beaches.

25. The **Eastern Desert Express** in Egypt offers scenic desert views on its way to the Red Sea.

Quiz Time: Multiple Choice Questions

1. What is the longest passenger train ride in the world?
A. Rocky Mountaineer
B. Indian Pacific
C. Trans-Siberian Railway
D. Orient Express

2. What country is home to the Glacier Express?
A. Canada
B. Switzerland
C. Norway
D. Japan

3. What famous train goes through the Channel Tunnel from London to Paris?
A. Shinkansen
B. Eurostar
C. Frecciarossa
D. Zephyr

✓ **MCQ Answer Key**

1 – C
2 – B
3 – B

Chapter 10: Train Disasters and Heroic Rescues

1. Trains are very safe, but accidents have happened throughout history.

2. The worst train disaster ever was the **2004 Sri Lanka tsunami train**, where over 1,700 people lost their lives.

3. In **1915**, a train in Mexico derailed on a steep slope, killing over 600 people.

4. The **Eschede disaster** in Germany (1998) was caused by a broken wheel and led to 101 deaths.

5. Train crashes often result from brake failure, speeding, or miscommunication.

6. In 2013, a train in Spain derailed after taking a curve at twice the speed limit.

7. In 1984, a toxic gas leak from a train in India affected thousands of people.

8. Heroic engineers have sometimes stayed at their controls to save lives.

9. In 1907, a New York subway motorman stopped a runaway train just in time.

10. Special sensors and brakes today help prevent accidents.

11. Trains now have **"dead man's switches"** that stop the train if the driver becomes unresponsive.

12. In 1995, a conductor in Canada guided his damaged freight train safely for 12 miles to

avoid a town.

13. Firefighters and rescue crews are trained to handle railway emergencies.

14. In Japan, after the 2011 earthquake, all bullet trains automatically stopped and prevented crashes.

15. Many train stations have **emergency buttons** and **safety zones**.

16. Railway crossings are marked with lights and gates to protect cars and pedestrians.

17. In 1952, two trains collided at high speed in London's Harrow station, leading to major safety reforms.

18. The **Lac-Mégantic disaster** in Canada (2013) caused a fire that destroyed much of the town.

19. Some survivors of train crashes have become safety advocates and heroes.

20. Today's trains are monitored by satellites and control centers.

21. Robots are used to inspect damaged tracks after disasters.

22. In some cases, animals on the tracks have caused accidents—like herds of cows or deer.

23. Train drivers often undergo emergency simulation training.

24. Many lives have been saved by the quick thinking of train crews.

25. Every accident teaches engineers new ways to make trains safer than before.

Quiz Time: Multiple Choice Questions

1. What is one cause of major train accidents?
A. Too many passengers
B. Wrong ticketing
C. Brake failure
D. Dirty windows

2. What stopped Japan's bullet trains during the 2011 earthquake?
A. Power outage
B. Manual brakes
C. Automatic safety system
D. Shouting from passengers

3. What is a "dead man's switch"?

A. A backup light
B. An emergency lever
C. A device that stops the train if the driver is unresponsive
D. A hidden key for conductors

✓ **MCQ Answer Key**

1 – C
2 – C
3 – C

Chapter 11: Animal Passengers and Funny Incidents

1. In Japan, a cat named **Tama** became the official station master of a train station—complete with a tiny hat!

2. Dogs have been known to ride trains by themselves and return home safely.

3. In Moscow, some stray dogs ride the subway daily to find food in the city.

4. Pigeons sometimes hop on trains in search of crumbs or warmth.

5. In one funny case, a raccoon caused a delay by sneaking into a train car!

6. A curious cow once blocked a train track in India for over an hour.

7. In Australia, a kangaroo once made it onto a platform and had to be gently guided out.

8. Police once stopped a train because a goat was riding on the roof!

9. In Thailand, monkeys have been spotted hopping on moving trains.

10. Some zoo animals, like giraffes and elephants, are moved by train during relocations.

11. Trains have transported **bees, horses, pigs, and even lions** under expert care.

12. A baby panda was once moved by bullet train in China to reduce travel stress.

13. Guide dogs are welcome passengers on most city trains around the world.

14. In some places, farmers take chickens and ducks on trains to market.

15. A family's pet parrot escaped its cage and rode a train two towns away!

16. One train delay in Canada was caused by a curious bear on the tracks.

17. In Scotland, a sheep boarded a train and sat peacefully until the next stop.

18. Conductors often have funny stories about lost pets, surprise animals, and odd behavior.

19. One engineer had to stop the train when a family of ducks refused to leave the track.

20. In Norway, reindeer sometimes cross the tracks in herds, requiring alert drivers.

21. Snakes have been found hiding under train seats—Alhamdulellah it is rare!

22. An ostrich once chased a train along a rural African railway.

23. Train mascots in costumes (like pandas or rabbits) often greet kids at stations.

24. Trains that visit farms or parks sometimes have animal petting zones onboard.

25. No matter the species, animals and trains create unforgettable moments!

Quiz Time: Multiple Choice Questions

1. What kind of animal became a train station master in Japan?
A. Dog
B. Cat
C. Parrot
D. Monkey

2. Which animals ride the subway in Moscow to find food?
A. Cats
B. Foxes
C. Dogs
D. Birds

3. What happened in Canada that caused a train delay?
A. Heavy snow
B. Bear on the tracks
C. Broken light
D. Lost suitcase

✓ MCQ Answer Key

1 – B
2 – C
3 – B

Chapter 12: Train Technology – Wheels, Tracks & Signals

1. Train wheels are made of **solid steel** to handle heavy weight and friction.

2. They have a special **flange**, or inner rim, to help stay on the track.

3. Train tracks are made from **hardened steel rails** placed on wooden or concrete ties.

4. **Ballast**—a layer of crushed stone—holds the track steady and drains rainwater.

5. Most train tracks are spaced **4 feet 8.5 inches (1,435 mm)** apart—this is called "standard gauge."

6. Some countries use **narrow gauge** tracks for mountain routes.

7. Train wheels don't turn separately like car wheels—they're locked on the same axle.

8. When a train turns, the wheel rims help adjust by sliding slightly across the rail.

9. Modern tracks use **welded rails**, which are smoother and reduce noise.

10. **Switches** (or turnouts) allow trains to move from one track to another.

11. **Signals** use lights and signs to tell train engineers when to stop, go, or slow down.

12. Red means stop, yellow means caution, and green means go—just like traffic lights!

13. Train brakes are controlled by **compressed air systems**.

14. Some trains use **dynamic brakes**, which turn the engine into a generator to slow down.

15. **Electric trains** draw power from overhead wires or rails called third rails.

16. Train stations often have **track indicators** showing where each train will arrive.

17. High-speed trains need extra-straight tracks and banked curves for safety.

18. **Track maintenance vehicles** check and repair rails regularly.

19. **Sensors** are placed on tracks to detect broken rails or obstacles.

20. **Automatic train control systems** help trains maintain safe distances.

21. Trains have **horns and bells** to warn people near tracks.

22. Some advanced trains now use **GPS and satellite tracking**.

23. **Remote-controlled switches** are operated from central command rooms.

24. Train couplers connect cars with tight locks that don't come loose.

25. Today's train technology is faster, safer, and more efficient than ever!

Quiz Time: Multiple Choice Questions

1. What is the purpose of a flange on a train wheel?
A. Make the wheel look fancy
B. Help the train speed up
C. Keep the wheel on the track
D. Create sparks

2. What does a red signal light mean for a train?
A. Go faster
B. Stop

C. Slow down
D. Turn

3. What powers electric trains?
A. Gas
B. Coal
C. Batteries
D. Overhead wires or third rails

✓ MCQ Answer Key

1 – C
2 – B
3 – D

Chapter 13: Famous Train Stations

1. **Grand Central Terminal** in New York City is one of the most famous train stations in the world.

2. It has a beautiful ceiling painted with **stars and constellations**.

3. Over **750,000 people** pass through Grand Central each day!

4. **Tokyo Station** serves hundreds of bullet trains daily.

5. The station in **Zurich, Switzerland**, has shops and restaurants.

6. **St. Pancras International** in London connects England to France via the **Eurostar**.

7. **Chhatrapati Shivaji Terminus** in Mumbai is a UNESCO World Heritage Site.

8. The **Beijing South Railway Station** is one of the largest and busiest in the world.

9. **Gare du Nord** in Paris is the busiest station in Europe.

10. **Berlin Hauptbahnhof** is a huge glass station with multiple levels of tracks.

11. The station in **Lhasa, Tibet**, is one of the world's highest at 11,450 feet (3,490 meters).

12. **Union Station** in Washington, D.C., features Roman-style architecture and gold leaf ceilings.

13. The **Kyoto Station** in Japan has a futuristic design with skywalks and escalators.

14. **São Bento Station** in Portugal has walls covered in **blue-and-white tile murals**.

15. **Helsinki Central** has a unique clock tower and giant stone statues.

16. **Melbourne's Flinders Street Station** has been a landmark since 1910.

17. **Amsterdam Centraal** sits by canals and offers boat-train transfers.

18. **Madrid Atocha Station** has a tropical garden inside the terminal!

19. **Toronto's Union Station** is Canada's busiest and connects to subways and buses.

20. The **Shinjuku Station** in Tokyo is the world's busiest, with over **3 million people** daily!

21. **Antwerp Central** in Belgium is often called the "Railway Cathedral" for its grand beauty.

22. **Rome Termini** serves trains heading all over Italy and beyond.

23. **Oslo Central Station** has modern designs and digital ticket counters.

24. Many train stations now have **automated ticket machines** for faster service.

25. Some major stations even have **hotels and gyms** inside!

Quiz Time: Multiple Choice Questions

1. Which train station is known for its starry ceiling?
A. Union Station
B. Grand Central Terminal
C. Kyoto Station
D. Gare du Nord

2. What is the busiest train station in the world?
A. Shinjuku Station
B. Beijing South
C. St. Pancras International
D. Zurich Central

3. What's special about São Bento Station in Portugal?
A. It's underground
B. It has moving floors
C. Its walls are covered in tiles
D. It floats on water

✓ MCQ Answer Key

1 – B
2 – A
3 – C

Chapter 14: Ice, Snow, and Mountain Rails

1. Trains operate in **extreme cold** in places like Siberia, Alaska, and northern Canada.

2. **Snowplow trains** are used to clear tracks after heavy snowstorms.

3. In Japan, snow walls along some tracks reach over **20 feet (6 meters)** high in winter.

4. The **Glacier Express** in Switzerland climbs high snowy mountains using special gears.

5. In Norway, trains run through icy tunnels and frozen fjords.

6. The **White Pass & Yukon Route** crosses snow-covered mountains between the U.S. and Canada.

7. Tracks in cold regions are built with **extra strength** to handle freezing temperatures.

8. **Mountain trains** often use a system called **rack-and-pinion** to grip steep slopes.

9. The **Darjeeling Himalayan Railway** in India winds through foggy hills and tea farms.

10. The **Qinghai–Tibet Railway** crosses the Tibetan Plateau and reaches over **16,000 feet (4,800 m)** in altitude.

11. Trains at high altitudes carry **oxygen supplies** for passengers.

12. Some train windows are **triple-glazed** to keep out icy winds.

13. Rail workers wear insulated gear to stay safe in freezing weather.

14. **Avalanche shields** are placed over tracks in the mountains to stop snow from burying trains.

15. **Snow sheds** are tunnels built just to protect tracks from heavy snow.

16. Trains in snowy areas use **heated rails** to stop ice buildup.

17. The **Bernina Express** crosses the Alps without a single tunnel—it climbs using spiral tracks instead!

18. In Canada, special locomotives are used to maintain traction in deep snow.

19. Some mountain trains move at **very slow speeds** for safety.

20. The **Himalayan Toy Train** runs on narrow-gauge tracks through misty hills.

21. In Alaska, freight trains continue to run all year—even in blizzards.

22. Mountain routes often have **many bridges and tunnels** to handle rough terrain.

23. Some trains offer **glass-roof cars** to let riders see snowy peaks above.

24. Train tracks in cold climates are checked often for cracks from freezing and thawing.

25. Whether crossing glaciers or frozen forests, mountain trains are built tough!

Quiz Time: Multiple Choice Questions

1. What do snowplow trains do?
A. Carry food
B. Plow roads

C. Clear snow from tracks
D. Heat up tracks

2. What is used on steep mountain railways to prevent slipping?
A. Sand
B. Extra wheels
C. Rack-and-pinion system
D. Jet engines

3. Which train travels the snowy Alps without using tunnels?
A. Glacier Express
B. Himalayan Toy Train
C. Bernina Express
D. Rocky Mountaineer

✓ MCQ Answer Key

1 – C
2 – C
3 – C

Chapter 15: Eco-Friendly and Solar Trains

1. Trains are one of the **most energy-efficient** ways to travel long distances.

2. Electric trains produce **less pollution** than cars or airplanes.

3. Many countries are replacing old diesel trains with **electric trains**.

4. Some trains run on **solar power**, using panels on the roof or along the tracks.

5. The first fully solar-powered train began operating in **Australia** in 2017.

6. Solar panels provide clean energy from the sun, reducing the need for fuel.

7. **Hydrogen-powered trains** produce only water vapor as exhaust.

8. These trains store energy in special **hydrogen fuel cells**.

9. Germany and the UK are already testing and using hydrogen trains.

10. Some stations use **wind power** to generate electricity for train systems.

11. In the Netherlands, electric trains are powered entirely by **wind energy**.

12. Regenerative braking systems can **recycle energy** every time a train slows down.

13. Green trains often use **lightweight materials** to save energy.

14. Trains with **aerodynamic designs** use less fuel by cutting through air more easily.

15. Engineers work to reduce **noise and vibration** to protect wildlife near tracks.

16. Some train systems recycle **waste heat** to power buildings.

17. Modern engines produce less smoke and use **cleaner fuels**.

18. Electric trains in some countries get power from **hydropower dams**.

19. Charging stations along the track help electric trains stay powered.

20. **Biodiesel** is used in some trains—fuel made from plants or recycled oil.

21. Trains can carry **hundreds of people** in one trip, reducing traffic on the roads.

22. New smart trains are built to turn off unused lights or systems to **save energy**.

23. Companies are investing in **green train stations** with plants and solar roofs.

24. Reducing train weight and improving wheel design also cuts down fuel use.

25. Eco-friendly trains are helping the planet by making travel cleaner and smarter!

Quiz Time: Multiple Choice Questions

1. What kind of energy do solar-powered trains use?
A. Wind
B. Diesel
C. The sun
D. Water

2. What is special about hydrogen-powered trains?
A. They have no brakes
B. They float
C. They produce only water vapor
D. They carry oil

3. Which country powers its electric trains entirely with wind energy?
A. Canada
B. Netherlands
C. China
D. Brazil

✓ **MCQ Answer Key**

1 – C
2 – C
3 – B

Chapter 16: The Future of Trains – Hovering and Flying?

1. Future trains may no longer need wheels—they could **hover using magnets**!

2. These are called **Maglev trains**—short for "magnetic levitation."

3. Maglev trains float slightly above the tracks using powerful magnetic fields.

4. Because they don't touch the track, there's **no friction**, so they go faster and smoother.

5. Japan's Maglev has reached **375 mph (603 km/h)** in test runs.

6. These trains are also **quiet**, because they don't create much noise.

7. China is building long Maglev lines to connect its biggest cities.

8. Engineers are also working on **Hyperloop systems**, where trains move in vacuum tubes.

9. Hyperloop trains could reach speeds over **700 mph (1,127 km/h)**!

10. Vacuum tubes remove air, so there's almost no resistance inside.

11. Hyperloop pods ride on **air cushions or magnets**, not wheels.

12. Some test Hyperloop tracks have already been built in the U.S. and the UAE.

13. In the future, trains might run **underground in giant tubes**, shooting between cities in minutes.

14. Trains of the future will use **AI and smart computers** to control everything safely.

15. Touchscreen controls and real-time updates will guide passengers easily.

16. New materials like **carbon fiber** may make trains lighter and faster.

17. Some futuristic trains are being designed with **self-cleaning interiors**.

18. Engineers are testing **drone-train hybrids** for small cargo deliveries.

19. Trains might one day glide **over water** using magnetic systems.

20. Underground trains may be powered by **kinetic energy** from braking.

21. Future train windows might be digital screens that show scenery or maps.

22. Solar tracks could be built directly into the railway to power the train.

23. In smart cities, trains will be synced with **driverless buses and cars**.

24. People may soon book train rides using just **face recognition or fingerprints**.

25. Whether flying, hovering, or riding in tubes, the trains of tomorrow will be fast, clean, and high-tech!

Quiz Time: Multiple Choice Questions

1. What does "Maglev" stand for?
A. Magnetic Level
B. Magnetic Levitation
C. Magnet Lift
D. Mag-Leap Vehicle

2. What is special about Hyperloop trains?
A. They float on water

B. They use horses
C. They move in vacuum tubes
D. They only carry food

3. How fast could Hyperloop trains go?
A. 200 mph
B. 400 mph
C. 600 mph
D. 700+ mph

✅ **MCQ Answer Key**

1 – B
2 – C
3 – D

Chapter 17: Train Travel Tips and Safety Facts for Kids

1. Always **stand behind the yellow line** while waiting for a train at the station.

2. Never try to **cross the tracks**, even if you don't see a train—use the bridge or underpass.

3. Only **board trains when they've come to a full stop** and doors have opened.

4. Hold an adult's hand when getting on or off crowded trains.

5. Keep your **belongings close** and out of the aisle during travel.

6. If seated near a door, don't lean on it—it may open or close automatically.

7. Use **inside voices** on the train so everyone can enjoy the ride.

8. Do not put hands, arms, or heads out of windows—even if they're open.

9. Most trains have **emergency brakes**—use them only in real emergencies.

10. Never run or play near tracks or platforms.

11. If traveling alone, stay near other passengers or alert train staff if unsure.

12. Many trains have **security cameras and conductors** to keep passengers safe.

13. Always keep your **ticket or travel card** with you until the ride ends.

14. When using the restroom on a train, hold onto handrails if the train is moving.

15. If a train stops in a tunnel, remain calm and **wait for announcements**.

16. Report any lost items to station staff or the train conductor.

17. Most stations have **lost and found** offices for misplaced belongings.

18. In case of emergencies, look for **exit signs** and follow crew instructions.

19. Stay alert at train crossings—never try to beat a train.

20. Obey all signs, lights, and announcements while on or near trains.

21. Wear **bright clothing** or reflective gear when around trains in low light.

22. Be patient during delays—train safety always comes first.

23. Don't climb on stopped trains—they can move suddenly and are very heavy.

24. If you feel unwell, let a train worker or adult know immediately.

25. Train travel is safe and fun when you **follow the rules and stay alert**!

Quiz Time: Multiple Choice Questions

1. What should you do while waiting for a train at the platform?
A. Stand close to the edge
B. Jump up and down
C. Stand behind the yellow line
D. Sit on the tracks

2. What should you do if a train stops in a tunnel?
A. Scream loudly
B. Try to get out
C. Stay calm and wait for instructions
D. Call the driver

3. When is it okay to play on train tracks?
A. During the day
B. On holidays
C. Never
D. If your friend says it's safe

✓ MCQ Answer Key

1 – C
2 – C
3 – C

Chapter 18: Mini Train Challenges, Records, and World Trivia

1. The **smallest working train model** in the world fits on a **coin** and can still move!

2. The **longest toy train track** ever built was over **2 miles (3.2 km)** long.

3. Some kids build model train worlds with **tiny towns, people, and mountains**.

4. In Germany, **Miniatur Wunderland** is the world's largest model railway display.

5. It has **over 50 trains** running at once through miniature cities and landscapes.

6. The world's **steepest rack railway** is the Pilatus Railway in Switzerland.

7. The **fastest LEGO train** was built by hobbyists and hit **6.5 mph (10.5 km/h)**!

8. The **world's largest steam locomotive** is called **Big Boy**—over 132 feet (40 meters) long.

9. The **oldest still-operating steam train** is over 150 years old.

10. One train in India crosses **over 1,000 bridges** on its route!

11. The **heaviest cargo ever pulled** by a train weighed nearly **100,000 tons**.

12. A **solar-powered toy train** built by kids once ran for 24 hours nonstop.

13. Japan's bullet trains are so smooth, people can **stand coins upright** on the tray table.

14. A train in Switzerland passes through a **spiral tunnel** inside a mountain!

15. The **coldest temperature** a train has ever run in was **−60°F (−51°C)**.

16. The world's **highest-altitude train station** is **Tanggula Station** in Tibet.

17. In the U.S., the **California Zephyr** crosses **seven different states** in one ride.

18. Some freight trains have **three or more engines** at the front and back to pull heavy loads.

19. **Bullet trains** are so punctual that even **a 30-second delay** makes the news.

20. In the Netherlands, trains are powered completely by **wind energy**.

21. **Animals like cats, dogs, and even goats** have made surprise appearances on trains.

22. The **Eurostar** crosses under the sea through the **Channel Tunnel**.

23. Trains are a **key part of the economy**, moving goods faster than ships or trucks.

24. Many countries are now building **faster, cleaner, and smarter** train systems.

25. No matter the size—from tiny models to massive freight trains—trains keep the world moving!

Quiz Time: Multiple Choice Questions

1. What's the name of the world's largest steam locomotive?
A. Iron Giant
B. Big Thunder
C. Big Boy
D. Super Steam

2. Which place is home to the world's largest model train exhibit?
A. Tokyo Station

B. Miniatur Wunderland
C. Union Station
D. Trainorama

3. How many states does the California Zephyr cross?
A. 3
B. 5
C. 7
D. 10

✅ **MCQ Answer Key**

1 – C
2 – B
3 – C

Bonus Chapter: The Ultimate Train Trivia Challenge!

15 Fun MCQs to Test Your Train Brain

1. What kind of train runs on magnets and does not touch the track?
A. Hyperloop

B. Diesel Train
C. Maglev
D. Glacier Express

2. Which train route crosses the snowy Canadian Rockies with beautiful views?
A. The Ghan
B. Coast Starlight
C. Rocky Mountaineer
D. Eurostar

3. What is the part of the train wheel that keeps it from sliding off the track?
A. Hubcap
B. Axle
C. Flange
D. Gear

4. Which country uses wind energy to power its entire electric train system?
A. Germany
B. Netherlands
C. Sweden
D. USA

5. What do train engineers use to control the train's speed and braking?
A. Switchboard
B. Joystick
C. Levers and knobs
D. Steering wheel

6. Which famous train ride crosses over 1,000 bridges during its journey?
A. Indian Pacific
B. Durango & Silverton
C. Himalayan Express
D. A route in India

7. Where would you find the world's largest model railway exhibit?
A. France
B. China
C. Germany
D. Canada

8. Which train technology uses vacuum tubes for super-fast travel?
A. Solar train
B. Maglev
C. Hyperloop
D. Electric tram

9. What's used underneath train tracks to hold them in place and drain water?
A. Cement
B. Tar
C. Ballast
D. Gravel bags

10. What is the name of Japan's high-speed rail system?
A. KTX
B. TGV

C. ICE
D. Shinkansen

11. Which mountain train in Switzerland climbs without using tunnels?
A. Pilatus Railway
B. Bernina Express
C. Glacier Express
D. Oslo Rail

12. What kind of train once carried zoo animals like elephants and giraffes?
A. Cargo shuttle
B. Tourist express
C. Livestock train
D. Animal transport train

13. Which city has the world's busiest train station with over 3 million daily users?
A. New York
B. Paris
C. Tokyo
D. Beijing

14. What do engineers use to switch a train from one track to another?
A. Gearbox
B. Paddle
C. Turnout or switch
D. Lever brake

15. Which futuristic train system may allow travel at speeds over 700 mph?
A. TGV
B. Hyperloop
C. MetroJet
D. UltraRail

✓ **Bonus Chapter Answer Key**

1 – C
2 – C
3 – C
4 – B
5 – C
6 – D
7 – C
8 – C
9 – C
10 – D
11 – B
12 – D
13 – C
14 – C
15 – B

☐ THANK YOU!

Dear Reader (and Awesome Train Fan!),

Thank you for hopping aboard and reading *444+ Fun and Fascinating Train Facts for Kids!* I truly appreciate your support and hope this book sparked curiosity, laughter, and learning with every page turn.

WHY YOUR REVIEW MATTERS

As an independent author, I don't have a big team or ads behind me—**what truly keeps books like this rolling are kind readers like you**.

Your honest review helps parents, teachers, and train-loving kids discover this fun and educational book. Just a few words can go a long way in helping other families find it.

> Even a short review—like what your child's favorite chapter was—can make a huge difference!

HOW TO LEAVE A REVIEW (Takes 60 Seconds!)

It's super easy:

1. Open your phone camera

2. Scan this QR code

3. Tap "Leave a Review" on Amazon

https://shorturl.at/x3cz0

(Start Reading)

YOUR SUPPORT = MORE FUN BOOKS

Every single review helps me continue writing clean, high-quality, educational books that inspire curiosity in young readers—without screens or distractions.

Enjoyed this ride?
 Then leave a review and help keep the train of learning to go for others!

✉☐ **Claim Your FREE Bonus Workbook**
Printable tools, I prayers, and progress charts to strengthen your marriage.

subscribepage.io/1YFjfB

About the Author: The Mind Behind the Initiative of Laughter and Learning

What if the smallest choice—like picking up this book—could change your child's world forever? That's the mission Dr. Rabea Hadi has embraced: turning curiosity into confidence, laughter into learning, and simple moments into lifelong memories. As the creative force behind many of the family-friendly bestsellers, Dr. Rabea crafts books that aren't just entertaining—they're transformative.

But why? What drives someone to write book after book filled with joy, humor, and values that parents trust? It all began in a career built on listening to stories—the real kind. Stories of resilience, struggles, and triumphs from patients who taught Dr. Rabea a profound truth: the human mind craves connection, laughter, and a sense of purpose. Inspired by those lessons, Dr. Rabea began weaving them into books that help families grow closer while exploring the wonders of the world.

Are you ready to give your child an edge in life? Dr. Rabea doesn't just write books—they create experiences that bring families together, spark curiosity, and foster mental resilience. Every story is designed to entertain, educate, and empower, ensuring your child builds not just knowledge, but confidence and joy.

Don't stop here. The adventure continues. Want possible exclusive content, behind-the-scenes insights, and early access to new releases? Subscribe to ChooseYourQuest.net, and form a growing community of readers who know that the right book can change everything.

The question isn't whether you should join—it's whether you can afford to miss out. Go to ChooseYourQuest.net now and take the first step in a journey of knowledge, laughter, and family connection?

"The Oneness"

In the vast expanse of sky and sea,
Tawheed whispers, clear and free.
One Creator, the source of all,
No partner, no equal, no one to call.

The mountains rise, the rivers flow,
By His command, all things grow.
In every heartbeat, in every prayer,
His oneness is known, everywhere.

Tawheed is the light, the guiding star,
No matter how near, no matter how far.
In His name, we find our peace,
From Him alone, all worries cease.

Books for Teens & Adults

The Galaxy of Comedy Series (Enhanced Edition): A Hilarious Space Adventure Where Everything (and Everyone) Could Go Wrong

"Looking for adventure in the galaxy? You might want to pack an extra pair of socks."

The Galaxy of Comedy takes you on a wild ride where every alien encounter, malfunctioning gadget, and intergalactic diner debacle could be your last—or at least, your most ridiculous. Follow our reluctant lab assistant hero who accidentally triggers a galaxy-hopping portal, **launching them into a universe full of quirky characters, laugh-out-loud mishaps, and a surprisingly epic quest.**

The Galaxy of Comedy is **one of the funniest books** `I've ever read! Reader review,` ★★★★★

Choose Your Quest: The Illustrated Interactive Series 6-in-1 Box Set: Thrilling Adventures In Fantasy, Sci-Fi, Historical Fiction and Thriller – Endless Choices, Multiple Endings, YOU Decide!

6 Books. Fun Adventures. YOU Control the Story.

Get ready for the ultimate reading experience with Choose Your Quest: The Complete 6-Book Interactive Adventure Omnibus. Perfect for fans of choose your own adventure (CYOA) stories, this thrilling collection puts YOU in control of the story, written entirely in immersive 2nd person POV.

Here's What Readers Are Saying:

"Just like the ones I used to read when I was a kid! … Thank you for the trip down memory lane :) **PLEASE MAKE MORE!**" – Reader reviewer

"**Wow, wow, wow!!! This is a must-read**... It will infuse life in you immediately!" – Reader reviewer

"**How come nobody thought of this before?!!!** This is a great method of interactive reading... Love it!" – Reader reviewer

"This turned self-help into a fun journey. Navigating through scenarios **felt like an epic quest!**" – Reader reviewer

Get The Ebook

Choose Your Quest: The Dwarven Jester Spy: An Interactive Hilarious High Fantasy Espionage Adventure

Can a jester become a master spy, or will his jokes get him killed?

In this interactive fantasy adventure, YOU take on the role of a quick-witted dwarven jester, secretly hired by the mysterious Group. But what begins as a routine mission quickly spirals into an epic conspiracy that could plunge entire kingdoms into chaos. Armed with nothing but your humor, a few tricks up your sleeve, and a sarcastic talking skull, you must navigate political intrigue, treacherous traps, and ridiculous enemies.

Each decision you make takes you down a unique path. Will you outsmart your foes or get caught in a deadly game of lies?

You decide! But be warned, one wrong step and the path of the realm (and your life) could hang in the balance.

- An Epic High-Fantasy World filled with orcs, elves, and dwarves, where humor is your best weapon.
- Hilarious Characters like the sarcastic talking skull and the eccentric figures you meet along the way.
- Multiple Endings depending on the choices you make, giving the book endless replayability.
- Perfect for Fantasy and Comedy Lovers who enjoy interactive, laugh-out-loud storytelling!

Fiction for Children

Uplifting Stories for Children 6-8 (10 books)

Welcome to the Uplifting Stories for Children series—**a collection of fun, heartwarming stories for children aged 6–8!** Each tale is filled with adventure, friendship, and important life lessons. From kindness and courage to teamwork and creativity, these stories focus on the **values** that help young readers grow into caring and confident individuals. With relatable characters and fun-filled journeys.

Join the adventure as our heroes discover that even the smallest acts of kindness can brighten the world around them. Whether it's helping a friend, learning from mistakes, or overcoming a challenge, The Series is all about positivity, values, and fun!

Are you ready to jump into a world of heartwarming adventures? Open a book, and let the fun begin! Get ready to laugh, learn, and make the world a brighter place—one story at a time. Let's go!

Daddy, You're My Hero: A Fun and Heartwarming Story About My Adventures with Dad, Laughter, and Noodles! Daddy, You're My Hero is a heartwarming and funny story about the special bond between a *little Asian girl and her father.* **Told through the eyes of 8-year-old Mei,** this charming tale follows her adventures with her dad as they navigate life's ups and downs with laughter, love, and noodle soup!

<u>Non-Fiction For Kids & Teens</u>

Fun Facts For Sports Kids (21 book series)

Do you know a young sports lover who's always hungry for more knowledge?

Whether they're just starting out, a casual fan, or a die-hard sports fanatic, this book series will satisfy their curiosity with a treasure trove of facts and trivia from the world of sports!

Inside each book of the *Fun Facts for Sports Kids* series, readers will discover:

- Hundreds of mind-blowing, fun, and jaw-dropping sports facts and trivia
- Unbelievable insights, from the science behind each sport to tales of epic comebacks, legendary players, and record-breaking feats

- A captivating layout that keeps readers engaged from cover to cover
- Unique chapters spanning player superstitions, famous fans, inspiring friendships, coaching insights, and more, tailored to each sport

Here's a sneak peek at some surprising facts you might find:

- Did you know that basketball was originally played with a soccer ball and peach baskets instead of hoops?
- Or, did you know that a marathon was once stopped by a herd of sheep crossing the path of the runners?
- Can you name the sport where athletes have to avoid hitting an underwater puck to the surface?

No matter which sport they love most, *Fun Facts for Sports Kids* is the perfect gift for the young sports fan in your life. So, if you know someone who can't get enough of sports, dive into a world of incredible facts that will amaze and inspire them!

Buy now to bring home the ultimate sports trivia experience?

Did You Know That Your Heart Beats Over 100,000 Times a Day or That Stars Can Be Different Colors?

Fun Facts For Kids 6-8 (17 books)

Scan here to buy The 444+ Fun Facts for Kids series—where every page is packed with incredible trivia about nature, space, anatomy, and more! Perfect for curious kids (and their parents) who love to explore, learn, and quiz themselves on amazing facts.

https://www.bookbub.com/authors/rabea-hadi

https://www.goodreads.com/author/list/50227090.Rabea_Hadi

Printed in Dunstable, United Kingdom